One-of-a-Kind Stamps and Crafts

KATHY ROSS

ILLUSTRATED BY NICOLE in den BOSCH

M Millbrook Press/Minneapolis

For Julianna and Ashlyn
Love, Grandma

Millbrook Press
A division of Lerner Publishing Group, Inc.
241 First Avenue North
Minneapolis, MN 55401 U.S.A.

Website address: www.lernerbooks.com

Library of Congress Cataloging-in-Publication Data

Ross, Kathy (Katharine Reynolds), 1948–
    One-of-a-kind stamps and crafts / by Kathy Ross ; illustrated by Nicole in den Bosch.
        p.   cm. — (Girl crafts)
    ISBN: 978–0–8225–9216–7 (lib. bdg. : alk. paper)
    1. Rubber stamp printing—Juvenile literature. 2. Handicraft for girls—Juvenile literature.
I. Bosch, Nicole in den. II. Title.
TT867.R67 2010
    761—dc22   2009020626

Manufactured in the United States of America
1 – VI – 12/15/2009

Contents

Dear Reader,

If you have used any of my craft books before, you already know that I do not think crafting should cost a lot. I am always looking for ways to have fun with crafting techniques without having to spend a great deal of money. I love to stamp, but rubber stamps can be expensive. This book is full of ideas for making your own stamps. You can use the stamps to decorate stationery, storage boxes, notebooks, picture frames—and even shoelaces!

Here are some things you should know before getting started.

- Stamps work best when mounted on a hard base. Blocks of wood are great stamp bases. If you do not have access to wood, try using corks, lids from spray cans or laundry detergent bottles, or plastic bottle caps for the stamp bases.

- If the stamp you make is thin, you might have trouble with some of the base around the stamp shape making a print when you do not want it to. To avoid this, mount the stamp on one or more layers of craft foam. Trim the extra foam from around the stamp. This will raise the stamp farther off the base and solve the problem.

- Try your stamp on scrap paper first, to make sure the print comes out the way you want it to.

When I was growing up, my sisters and I made a lot of our own fun. We were creative with the materials available to us. I hope this book inspires you to think creatively too!

Kathy Ross

Use this simple stamp to make all kinds of pictures.

Double Dot Stamp

Here is what you need:

unsharpened pencil

pony bead

white craft glue

ink pads

Here is what you do:

1. Glue the pony bead to the wood end of the pencil.

2. Use the eraser end to stamp a solid circle and the pony bead end to stamp a donut circle.

HINT: Make a separate stamp for each color of ink you want to use.

Stamp a group of dots to create a picture, to make a border around some artwork, or to decorate narrow items such as shoelaces and ribbons.

Buttons come in many different shapes and sizes. They can be used to create an endless variety of different prints.

Button Flower Stamp

Here is what you need:

variety of old buttons

white craft glue

scrap paper

ink pads

markers

old corks or small plastic bottle caps

pipe cleaners (optional)

Here is what you do:

1. If your button has a pattern or design on it, only the highest parts of the button will create a print. Try making prints on scrap paper from lots of different buttons. Then decide which ones make the best stamps.

2. Glue each button you choose to the end of a cork or the flat side of a bottle cap. This will create a handle that will make using the stamps much easier.

3. Use the button stamps to print flowers.

4. Use the markers to add stems and color to each flower.

HINT: For buttons with a loop on the back, you can use a piece of pipe cleaner as your handle. Thread a 4-inch (10-cm) piece of pipe cleaner through the loops. Then bring the two ends together, and twist to make a handle.

Use your button stamps to make your own designer note cards.

These quick and easy stamps make pictures that have a fuzzy look to them. Try it!

Pom-Pom Stamp

Here is what you need:

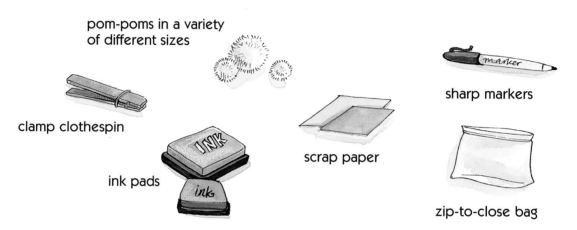

pom-poms in a variety of different sizes

clamp clothespin

ink pads

scrap paper

sharp markers

zip-to-close bag

Here is what you do:

1. Clamp the end of a clamp clothespin to one side of a pom-pom. This will be the handle. You can use the same clothespin and change the pom-pom when you need a different size or ink color.

2. Practice stamping different colors and sizes on the scrap paper. The circles will be fuzzy looking around the edges and solid in the middle.

3. Combine the pom-pom stamps to make simple pictures.

4. Use the markers to add details to the stamps.

5. Store the pom-poms in the zip-to-close bag.

HINT: Use a different pom-pom for each color of ink.

Pom-pom pictures make adorable gift tags.

Save those scraps of craft foam for this stamp idea.

Foam Shape Stamp

Here is what you need:

white craft glue

scissors

lids for bases

ink pads

pen or pencil

craft foam scraps

Here is what you do:

1. Draw a simple shape on the craft foam. The picture should be small enough to fit on a lid without hanging over.

2. Cut it out. If the craft foam is thin, cut two identical shapes and glue them together to make it thicker. (You can do this by cutting one shape out and then tracing around it on another piece of foam to make the second shape to cut.)

3. Glue the shape to the flat top of a lid to make the base.

4. Make lots of different shapes.

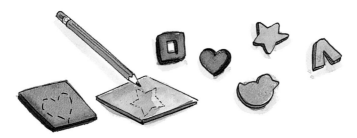

HINT: If you have a bag of precut foam shapes, these are perfect to use to create more stamps. How easy!

**Use permanent ink to stamp shapes on a balloon.
Blow it up, and see what happens.**

This is a "reverse" stamp. The print will leave an ink border around the picture you've carved.

Carved Foam Stamp

Here is what you need:

ink pads

white craft glue

scissors

craft foam

ballpoint pen

Here is what you do:

1. Use the pen to draw a small, simple picture on the craft foam.

2. Use the pen to carve out the lines of the picture without cutting all the way through the foam.

$3.$ Cut the foam in a square or circle around the picture.

$4.$ Cut five pieces of craft foam the same size and shape as the picture stamp.

$5.$ Glue the pieces in layers to the back of the stamp to make a "chunky" stamp.

HINT: If your print isn't coming out well, try using the end of a paper clip to carve your design a bit deeper.

You can stamp a set of unique party invitations in no time with this stamp.

These stamps are perfect for printing on curved surfaces.

Appliqué and Lace Stamps

Here is what you need:

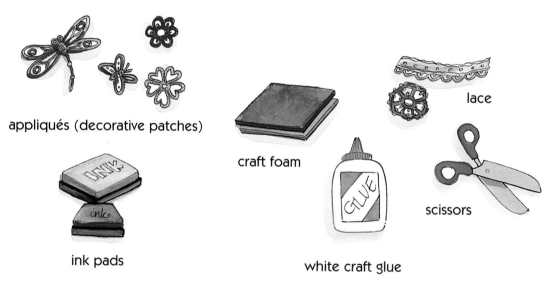

appliqués (decorative patches)

craft foam

lace

ink pads

white craft glue

scissors

Here is what you do to make an appliqué stamp:

1. Choose a small appliqué, or you may cut out part of a larger appliqué. The most common shapes are flowers and butterflies. Choose appliqués with well-defined edges.

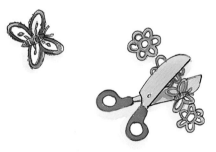

2. Cut a square of foam that is slightly larger than the appliqué shape. Glue the appliqué to the center of the piece of craft foam.

Here is what you do to make a lace stamp:

1. Glue a strip of lace to a piece of craft foam.

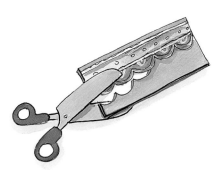

2. Trim the extra foam from around the lace. The foam is flexible and will allow the stamp to wrap around a curved surface to print.

HINT: Permanent ink is needed for the print to stay on surfaces other than paper.

Use the appliqué and lace stamps to print a pattern on a votive candle or a glass jar.

Use ball head pins to stamp a simple heart.

Ball Head Pin Heart Stamp

Here is what you need:

2½ to 3-inch (6- to 8-cm) Styrofoam ball

pencil

white craft glue

scissors

ink pads

ball head pins

cereal box cardboard

Here is what you do:

1. Cut about a third off one side of the Styrofoam ball, making a flat surface. Save the smaller piece for another project.

2. Use the pencil to trace around the flat side of the Styrofoam ball onto the cereal box cardboard.

3. Cut out the traced circle.

4. Draw a simple heart outline on the plain side of the cardboard.

5. Glue the printed side of the cardboard to the Styrofoam ball.

6. Press pins through the cardboard and into the Styrofoam ball in the shape of the heart. Keep the pins as close together as possible.

HINT: You may want to ask an adult to help you cut the Styrofoam.

**Make a gift bag by stamping hearts on a brown lunch bag.
Add a gift, and tie the top shut with ribbon or twine. Pretty!**

Craft sequins come in a variety of shapes and make excellent stamps.

Sequin Stamp

Here is what you need:

three or more of the same shape sequin

bottle caps or cork

white craft glue

embossed sequin (optional)

ink pads

Here is what you do:

1. Choose the shape sequin you want to use for your stamp. Glue at least three of the same sequin shape together to make a thicker shape.

2. Embossed sequins will give a more detailed stamp because they have designs that stand out from the flat surface. Because they tend to be thicker, you may be able to get a good print using just one sequin.

3. Glue the stacked sequin shapes or the embossed sequin to the flat top of the cap or cork.

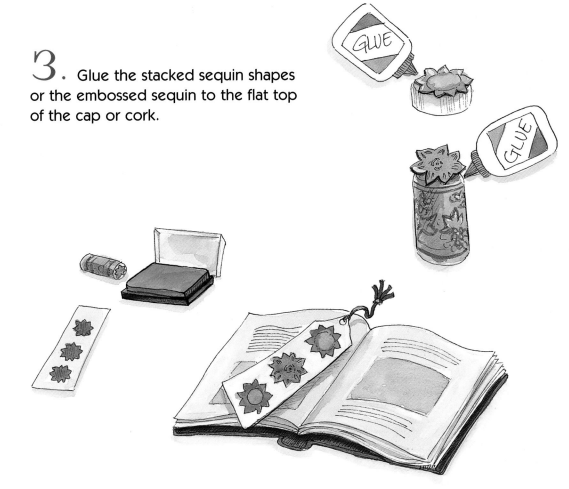

Print a 1½-inch x 6-inch (4- x 15-cm) strip of light cardboard with sequin stamps. Cover both sides of the strip with clear packing tape to protect it. Punch a hole in one end, and tie some yarn or thin ribbon through the hole. Now you have a one-of-a-kind bookmark.

Roller stamps make nice borders on notepaper and envelopes.

Roller Border Stamp

Here is what you need:

2½- to 3-inch (6- to 8-cm) Styrofoam ball

heavy rickrack (decorative sewing trim)

scissors

straight pins

ink pads

Here is what you do:

1. Cut a piece of rickrack to fit around the Styrofoam ball.

$2.$ Wrap the rickrack around the ball, and pin it so that the rickrack makes a continuous zigzag pattern.

$3.$ Roll the ball back and forth over the ink pad to cover all the rickrack with ink. Roll the inked ball over the paper you want to decorate.

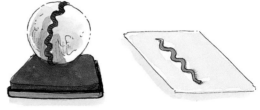

HINT: Look for other kinds of trim to use for stamping. You can use the same Styrofoam ball and just change the trim.

Make your own stationery by rolling this stamp down the left edge of plain paper.

Use odd pieces from a discarded jigsaw puzzle to stamp gift tags.

Puzzle Piece Stamp

Here is what you need:

empty plastic pill bottle or film container for each piece

markers

old puzzle pieces

white craft glue

collage materials such as wiggle eyes, ribbon bits, and craft foam

ink pads

Here is what you do:

1. Glue the colored side of the puzzle piece to the bottom of the film container or pill bottle.

2. Stamp the shape on paper.

3. Use collage materials and markers to make the stamped shape into a character such as a person, bird, or frog.

Have fun using different puzzle shapes to create your own group of unique characters and pictures.

Get lots of stamps in one with this idea.

Changing Stamp

Here is what you need:

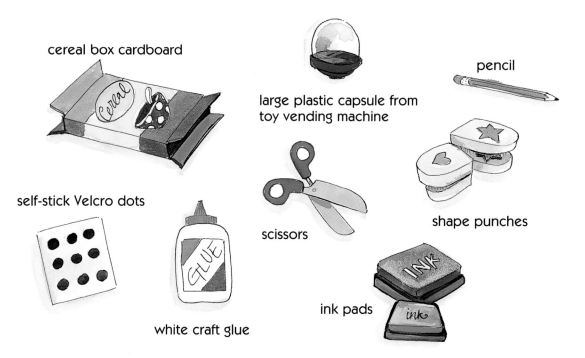

cereal box cardboard

large plastic capsule from
toy vending machine

pencil

self-stick Velcro dots

scissors

shape punches

white craft glue

ink pads

Here is what you do:

1. Take the hook side of one dot
pair. Stick the back of it on the center of
the plastic capsule lid.

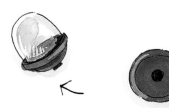

2. Use the shape punches to punch different shapes from the cereal box cardboard. You can also use the pencil to draw your own simple shapes and cut them out.

3. You will need at least three of each shape you make. (You can do this by cutting one shape out and then tracing around it on another piece of cardboard to make the second shape to cut.)

4. Glue the identical shapes together to make a thicker shape stamp.

5. Stick a piece of the fuzzy side of a Velcro dot to the back of each shape.

6. To use the stamp, choose the shape you want and stick it to the capsule lid by pressing the two sides of the Velcro together.

HINT: Store all your "changing stamps" inside the capsule.

Turn a set of plain labels into address labels, and use your new stamps to decorate them.

Plastic mesh adds a pattern to your stamp shapes.

Mesh Net Stamp

Here is what you need:

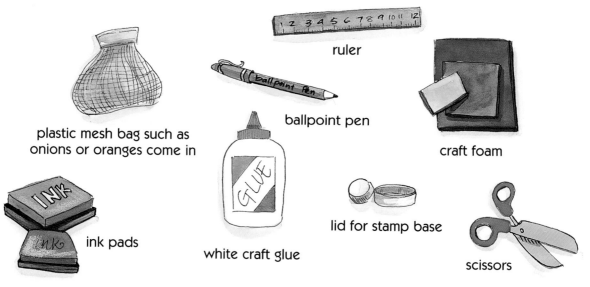

ruler

ballpoint pen

craft foam

plastic mesh bag such as
onions or oranges come in

lid for stamp base

ink pads

white craft glue

scissors

Here is what you do:

1. Use the pen to draw a simple 1- to
2-inch (2.5- to 5-cm) shape on the craft
foam. The mesh design looks especially
nice on an alligator, fish, or basket shape.

2. Cut out the shape.

3. Cut a piece of mesh, and glue it over the shape.

4. When the glue has dried, trim away the extra mesh around the shape.

5. Glue the shape, mesh side out, to the center of the top of the lid.

HINT: What else could you try gluing over a stamp shape to add a pattern? Maybe lace, crushed velvet, or a piece of paper doily would work. Try cutting a shape from the stiff plastic mesh used for needlework. Experiment!

You can add detail to your stamp. Try gluing a ribbon to a basket shape or putting wiggle eyes on a fish.

Make stamps of your favorite words.

Pipe Cleaner Word Stamp

Here is what you need:

pipe cleaners or sparkle stems

scrap paper

white craft glue

ink pads

sturdy block of wood or small box bottom

Here is what you do:

1. Use a pipe cleaner or sparkle stem to shape a continuous word in cursive writing. Keep the word smaller than your ink pad.

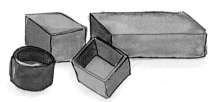

2. Glue the word BACKWARD to the block of wood or box bottom. The easiest way to do this is to place the word faceup on scrap paper. Then cover the base box or wood with glue, and press it down on the word.

HINT: Pipe cleaner and sparkle stem stamps will have different print textures, so you might want to try both kinds of stem material.

Pipe cleaner words are perfect for making cards and decorating boxes. Be sure to make a stamp of your own name!

Try this creative way to use glue!

White Glue Stamp

Here is what you need:

pencil

scrap paper

scissors

flat-topped lid or craft foam

plastic wrap

white craft glue

ink pads

Here is what you do:

1. Use the pencil and scrap paper to draw a simple design for the stamp you want to make.

2. Place the drawing under a piece of the plastic wrap.

3. Carefully trace the design using the squeeze bottle of white glue. Then fill in the picture using a thick covering of glue.

4. Let the glue dry completely.

5. Carefully peel the design off the plastic wrap.

6. Use scissors to even out the edges of the glue shape if needed.

7. Glue the design to a piece of craft foam or a lid.

8. If you glue the design to craft foam, you may want to glue three or more layers of foam to the stamp to make a thicker base.

9. Trim the foam around the glue picture to cut the design out, or leave a foam background around it.

HINT: Try making some glue stamps with and without the foam background around the stamp, and see which you like better.

Use your glue stamp to decorate 4-inch (10-cm) cardboard circles. Cover both sides of each circle with clear contact paper to make a set of coasters.

Small, flat objects make interesting stamps.

Coin Stamp

Here is what you need:

corks or plastic bottle caps

play coins

white craft glue

ink pads

scrap paper

Here is what you do:

1. Experiment with stamping the coins on scrap paper to see which side of each one makes the best print.

2. Glue each coin to the end of a cork or flat side of a cap with the side you want to print facing out.

HINT: Discarded flat jewelry and the flat "charms" used for scrapbooking make wonderful stamps. Wooden craft shapes make nice stamps too. Mount them as you would the coin stamps.

Ms. Parker
2 Main Street
Alpine, CA. 22311

Next time you send a letter, seal the envelope and then use your coin stamp over the seal. It will add an elegant touch to your correspondence!

Spell out messages with a set of letter stamps.

Carved Letter Stamp

Here is what you need:

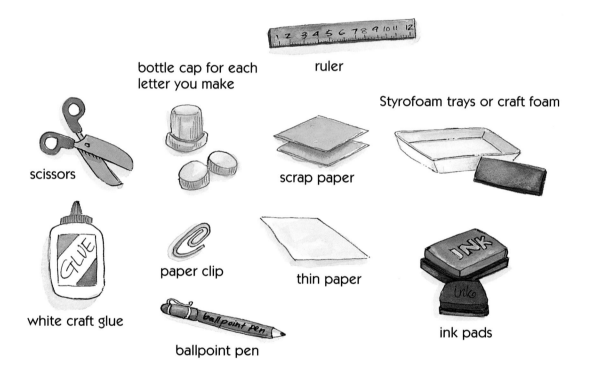

ruler

bottle cap for each
letter you make

Styrofoam trays or craft foam

scissors

scrap paper

white craft glue

paper clip

thin paper

ink pads

ballpoint pen

Here is what you do:

1. Cut a 1-inch (2.5-cm) circle from
the Styrofoam tray or craft foam for each
letter you want to make.

2. Use the pen to write the letter on thin paper. Press down so that you can see the letter on the back of the paper. Turn the paper over, and you'll see the letter backward. (Use this as a model to copy when drawing backward on the circle.)

3. Use the pen to draw the letter backward on the Styrofoam or foam circle. Press down and gently carve out the letter to get a good, clear stamp.

4. Test the letter by pressing it in the ink and printing it on scrap paper. If the letter is not clear, use the end of the paper clip to carve the letter deeper.

5. When you are happy with the print the letter makes, glue the back of the circle to a bottle cap.

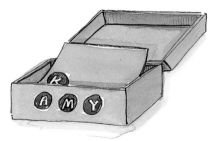

Make a box for your secret stuff, and use letter stamps to print your name on the front. You might also want to stamp a message such as "Keep Out."

Print textured shapes with this stamp idea.

Seed Bead Stamp

Here is what you need:

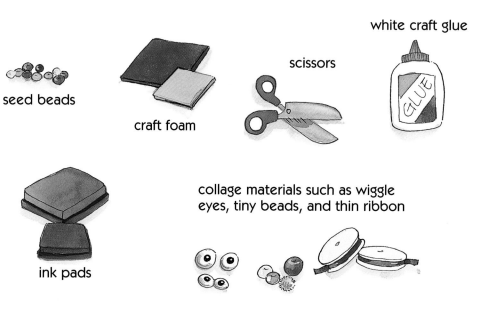

seed beads

craft foam

scissors

white craft glue

ink pads

collage materials such as wiggle eyes, tiny beads, and thin ribbon

Here is what you do:

1. Decide what kind of stamp shape you want to make. Seed beads work especially well for animal shapes and heads.

2. Cut a square of craft foam for the base of the stamp. You may want to add extra layers for strength.

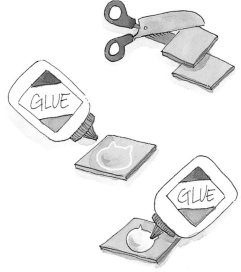

3. Use the glue to draw the shape you chose on the craft foam.

4. Fill in the shape with glue.

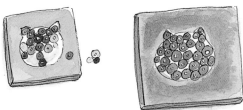

5. Cover the shape with a single layer of seed beads. Let the glue dry.

6. After you stamp, use collage materials to add details to the seed bead print shape.

HINT: Flatten the layer of beads on the glue to make an even surface to print from.

Make your own fancy stickers by stamping on a large white label. Cut the shape out, and decorate it with collage materials. To use the sticker, peel off the backing and stick!

Save a few flat-sided rubber bands for this project.

Rubber Band Stamp

Here is what you need:

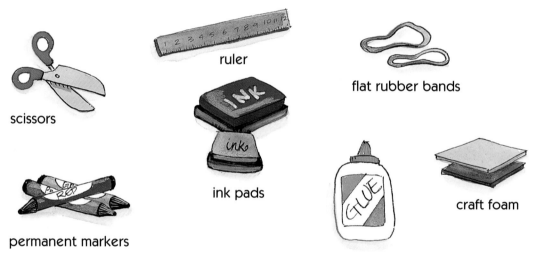

scissors

ruler

flat rubber bands

ink pads

permanent markers

white craft glue

craft foam

Here is what you do:

1. Cut a square of craft foam about 2 x 2 inches (5 x 5 cm) for the stamp base.

$2.$ Cut pieces of flat-sided rubber bands, and use the pieces to make a picture.

$3.$ Once you have arranged the pieces to make a picture that you like, glue the pieces to the craft foam square.

$4.$ When the glue has dried, trim away the extra foam around your shape.

HINT: This stamp will print well on a curved surface because of the thin, flexible foam base.

Try using your stamp with permanent ink to decorate some paper cups. Stamp the corner of several paper napkins to match the cups. You might want to color the picture with permanent markers. They make great gifts. Or use them to host a party!

This stamp will help you print wrapping paper quickly.

Cardboard Tube Roller Stamp

Here is what you need:

four cardboard
toilet tissue tubes

scissors

ink pads

sticky-backed foam
craft shapes

Here is what you do:

1. Cut down the side of each of three cardboard tubes.

2. Overlap the cut edges of the first cut tube to make it small enough to fit inside the fourth tube. Slide tube inside the uncut tube.

3. Roll up the next cut tube, and slide it inside the first two tubes.

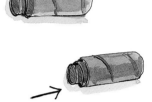

4. Roll up the last tube, and slide it inside the other tubes. This will make your roller sturdy.

5. Stick the foam shapes around the outside of the tube roller.

6. To use the roller stamp, roll it over the ink pad to cover all the shapes with ink. Then roll on paper surface to be printed.

HINT: If you do not have any sticky-backed foam shapes, cut your own shapes from craft foam and glue them to the roller.

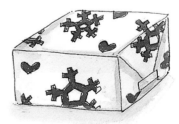

Tissue paper is easy to stamp on and makes great wrapping paper.

Small leaves make beautiful temporary stamps.

Leaf Stamp

Here is what you need:

craft foam

white craft glue

scissors

small leaf with defined veins on back

ink pads

Here is what you do:

1. Glue three pieces of craft foam together to make a thick base.

2. Glue the front of the leaf to the craft foam base.

3. When the glue has dried, trim away the extra craft foam.

HINT: Use different stamps for different seasons of the year.

Use permanent ink to print leaves on a square of plastic wrap. Press the other side of the wrap on a window. It will look as if leaves are on the window glass.

Make a shelf to store your ink pads.

Ink Pad Storage Shelf

Here is what you need:

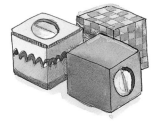

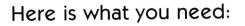

ruler

three square empty tissue boxes

scissors

craft paint and a paintbrush

white craft glue

colorful plastic straws

Here is what you do:

1. Cut the top square (with the opening for the tissues) out of one tissue box.

2. Turn the box on its side.

3. Cut the top and the bottom squares from the other two tissue boxes.

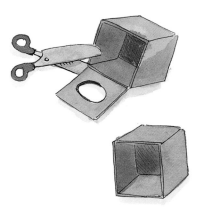

(continued)

43

4. Cut these two boxes in half by cutting front to back down the center of each side without the glued flaps.

5. This will give you four shelves, but you will only need three of them. Trim the sides of three of the shelves to about 1¼ inches (3 cm) tall.

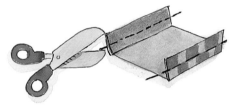

6. Paint the tissue box and the three shelves. Let them dry.

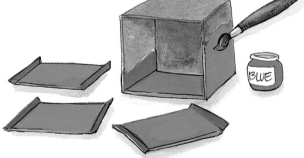

7. Glue the shelves into the open box, one on top of the other, by gluing the sides of each shelf to the inside of the box.

$8.$ Cut four 4¼-inch (11-cm) pieces of plastic straw.

$9.$ Cut up the length of each piece of straw to open it.

$10.$ Slip a straw over the front edge of each shelf opening for decoration. Secure each straw ledge with glue if needed.

HINT: Save the extra pieces of cardboard. You can use them to make some of the stamps and projects in this book! (See pages 16, 18, 24, and 30.)

Keep your ink pad shelf on your desk, so that you'll always be ready for stamping!

Make a box to store your stamp collection in.

Stamp Storage Box

Here is what you need:

sturdy box with lid

craft paint and a paintbrush

smaller cardboard jewelry boxes and lids

permanent ink pads

newspaper to work on

scissors

white craft glue

Here is what you do:

1. Arrange the smaller boxes and lids inside the larger box to form compartments for the stamps you will be storing. (The lids of the small boxes can also be used as compartments.) You can cut the boxes to the size you need to fit inside the larger box.

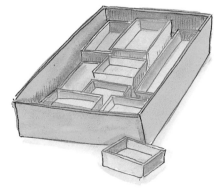

2. When you have the smaller boxes arranged the way you want them, glue them to the inside of the box.

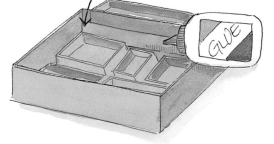

3. Working on the newspaper, paint the entire box and lid.

4. Decide which stamp or stamps you will keep in each compartment.

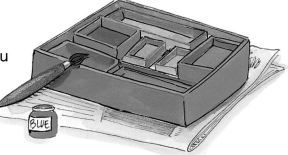

5. On the bottom of each compartment, make a print of the stamp or stamps you will store there. This way, you will quickly know where to put them away.

HINT: If you stamp a compartment and it is not a good print, you can easily fix it. Stamp the design on another piece of paper, cut it out, and glue it over the design you were not happy with.

Use some of your stamps to decorate the lid of the storage box.

About the Author

With more than one million copies of her books in print, Kathy Ross has written over fifty titles and her name has become synonymous with "top quality craft books." Following twenty-five years of developing nursery school programs and guiding young children through craft projects, Ross has authored many successful series, including *Crafts for Kids Who Are Learning about . . .*, *Girl Crafts*, and *All New Holiday Crafts for Kids*.